TESTIMONY
OF
THE HONORABLE J. RUSSELL GEORGE
TREASURY INSPECTOR GENERAL FOR TAX ADMINISTRATION
before the
COMMITTEE ON APPROPRIATIONS, SUBCOMMITTEE ON
FINANCIAL SERVICES AND GENERAL GOVERNMENT
UNITED STATES SENATE

"Review of the President's Fiscal Year 2017 Funding Request for the
Internal Revenue Service"
March 8, 2016

Chairman Boozman, Ranking Member Coons, and Members of the Subcommittee, thank you for the opportunity to testify on the Internal Revenue Service's (IRS) Fiscal Year (FY)[1] 2017 budget request, our recent work related to the most significant challenges currently facing the IRS, and the Treasury Inspector General for Tax Administration's (TIGTA) FY 2017 budget request.

TIGTA is statutorily mandated to provide independent audit and investigative services necessary to improve the economy, efficiency, and effectiveness of IRS operations, including the oversight of the IRS Chief Counsel. TIGTA's oversight activities are designed to identify high-risk systemic inefficiencies in IRS operations and to investigate exploited weaknesses in tax administration. TIGTA's role is critical in that we provide the American taxpayer with assurance that the approximately 86,000 IRS employees[2] who collected over $3.3 trillion in tax revenue, processed over 244 million tax returns, and issued more than $400 billion in tax refunds during FY 2015,[3] have done so in an effective and efficient manner while minimizing the risks of waste, fraud, or abuse.

TIGTA's Office of Audit (OA) reviews all aspects of the Federal tax administration system and provides recommendations to: improve IRS systems and operations; ensure the fair and equitable treatment of taxpayers; and detect and prevent waste, fraud, and abuse in tax administration. The OA places an emphasis on statutory

---

[1] The Federal Government's fiscal year begins on October 1 and ends on September 30.
[2] Total IRS staffing as of October 3, 2015. Included in the total are approximately 15,400 seasonal and part-time employees.
[3] IRS, *Management's Discussion & Analysis, Fiscal Year 2015*.

coverage required by the IRS Restructuring and Reform Act of 1998 (RRA 98)[4] and other laws, as well as on areas of concern raised by Congress, the Secretary of the Treasury, the Commissioner of Internal Revenue, and other key stakeholders. The OA has examined specific high-risk issues such as identity theft, refund fraud, improper payments, information technology, security vulnerabilities, complex modernized computer systems, tax collections and revenue, and waste and abuse in IRS operations.

TIGTA's Office of Investigations (OI) protects the integrity of the IRS by investigating allegations of IRS employee misconduct, external threats to IRS employees and facilities, and other attempts to impede or otherwise interfere with the IRS's ability to collect taxes. Since the summer of 2013, a significant part of the OI's workload has consisted of investigating a telephone impersonation scam in which approximately one million intended victims have received unsolicited telephone calls from criminals claiming to be IRS agents. The callers demand money under the guise of a tax liability from the victim. To date, over 5,400 victims have paid close to $29 million to these criminals. In addition, the OI investigates misconduct by IRS employees which manifests itself in many ways, including extortion, theft, taxpayer abuses, false statements, financial fraud, and identity theft. The Office of Investigations places a high priority on its statutory responsibility to protect all IRS employees located in over 670 facilities nationwide. In the last several years, threats directed at the IRS have remained the second largest component of the OI's work. Physical violence, harassment, and intimidation of IRS employees continue to pose challenges to the implementation of a fair and effective system of tax administration. The Office of Investigations is committed to ensuring the safety of IRS employees and the taxpayers who conduct business in IRS facilities.

TIGTA's Office of Inspections and Evaluations (I&E) provides responsive, timely, and cost-effective inspections and evaluations of challenging areas within the IRS, providing TIGTA with additional flexibility and capability to produce value-added products and services to improve tax administration. The I&E's work is not a substitute for audits and investigations. In fact, its findings may result in subsequent audits and/or investigations. Inspections are intended to monitor compliance with applicable law, regulation, and/or policy; assess the effectiveness and efficiency of programs and operations; and inquire into allegations of waste, fraud, abuse, and mismanagement. Evaluations, on the other hand, are intended to provide in-depth reviews of specific

---

[4] Pub. L. No. 105-206, 112 Stat. 685 (1998) (codified as amended in scattered sections of 2 U.S.C., 5 U.S.C. app., 16 U.S.C., 19 U.S.C., 22 U.S.C., 23 U.S.C., 26 U.S.C., 31 U.S.C., 38 U.S.C., and 49 U.S.C.).

management issues, policies, or programs. In the last year, the I&E has reviewed the IRS's process for disclosing taxpayers' Personally Identifiable Information and related tax information; performed an inspection of Taxpayer Assistance Centers; and reviewed requests for adaptive technology made by IRS employees with disabilities.

OVERVIEW OF THE IRS'S FY 2017 BUDGET REQUEST

The IRS is the largest component of the Department of the Treasury and has primary responsibility for administering the Federal tax system. The IRS's Strategic Plan guides program and budget decisions. In addition, the IRS has established a new investment process and created six strategic themes to guide its investment strategy and resource allocation. The IRS believes these themes align with existing Strategic Goals and Objectives and clearly articulate the strategic outcomes which the IRS seeks to achieve. The IRS's role is unique within the Federal Government in that it collects the revenue that funds the Government and administers the Nation's tax laws. It also works to protect Federal revenue by detecting and preventing the growing risk of fraudulent tax refunds and other improper payments.

To achieve these goals, the proposed FY 2017 IRS budget requests appropriated resources of approximately $12.3 billion.[5] The total appropriations amount is an increase of slightly more than $1 billion, or approximately 9.3 percent more than the FY 2016 enacted level of approximately $11.2 billion. A comparison of next year's request with the current budget is shown in Table 1. The budget request includes a net staffing increase of 3,231 full-time equivalents (FTE)[6] for a total of approximately 84,803 appropriated FTEs.

---

[5] The FY 2017 budget request also includes approximately $141 million from reimbursable programs, $45 million from non-reimbursable programs, $400 million from user fees, $385 million in available unobligated funds from prior years, and a transfer of $5 million to another agency for a total amount of $13.2 billion in available resources.
[6] A measure of labor hours in which one FTE is equal to eight hours multiplied by the number of compensable days in a particular fiscal year.

TABLE 1
IRS Fiscal Year 2017 Budget Request Increase
Over FY 2016 Enacted Budget
(in Thousands)

Appropriations Account	FY 2016 Enacted	FY 2017 Request	$ Change	% Change
Taxpayer Services	$2,333,376	$2,406,318	$72,942	3.1%
Enforcement	$4,864,936	$5,216,263	$351,327	7.2%
Operations Support	$3,746,688	$4,314,099	$567,411	15.1%
Business Systems Modernization	$290,000	$343,415	$53,415	18.4%
Total Appropriated Resources	$11,235,000	$12,280,095	$1,045,095	9.3%

Source: Treasury Inspector General for Tax Administration's analysis of the IRS's FY 2017 Budget Request, Operating Level Tables.

The three largest appropriation accounts are Taxpayer Services, Enforcement, and Operations Support. The Taxpayer Services account provides funding for programs that focus on helping taxpayers understand and meet their tax obligations, while the Enforcement account supports the IRS's examination and collection efforts. The Operations Support account provides funding for functions that are essential to the overall operation of the IRS, such as infrastructure and information services. Finally, the Business Systems Modernization account provides funding for the development of new tax administration systems and investments in electronic filing.

As shown above, the Operations Support appropriation request for FY 2017 has the highest increase at over $567 million (328 FTEs) compared to FY 2016. The two largest components of this increase are $153 million to implement changes to deliver tax credits and other requirements for the Patient Protection and Affordable Care Act and the Health Care and Education Reconciliation Act of 2010[7] (collectively referred to as the Affordable Care Act or ACA) and $92 million for the operations and maintenance on deployed Business Systems Modernization projects.

---

[7] Pub. L. No. 111-148, 124 Stat. 119 (2010) (codified as amended in scattered sections of the Internal Revenue Code and 42 U.S.C.), as amended by the Heath Care and Education Reconciliation Act of 2010, Pub. L. No. 111-152, 124 Stat. 1029.

KEY CHALLENGES FACING THE IRS

In this section of my testimony, I will discuss several of the most significant challenges now facing the IRS as it administers our Nation's tax laws.

TAXPAYER SERVICE

TIGTA continues to review the IRS's efforts to provide quality customer service and recommend areas of improvement. Although the IRS has implemented recommendations to better assist the American taxpayer, significant challenges remain. The IRS has made cuts in its traditional services, which has significantly affected a number of areas.

First, for the IRS toll-free lines,[8] there have been long customer wait times, resulting in abandoned calls, and customers redialing. Despite other available options, most taxpayers continue to use the telephone as the primary method to contact the IRS. For the 2015 Filing Season, as of May 2, 2015, the IRS reported that there were approximately 83.2 million attempts to contact the IRS by calling the various customer service toll-free telephone assistance lines. Assistors answered approximately 8.3 million calls and provided a 37.6 percent Level of Service[9] with a 23.5 minute Average Speed of Answer.[10] It should be noted that the reported Level of Service for the 2014 Filing Season was 70.8 percent.

For the 2016 Filing Season, as of February 27, 2016, the IRS reports that approximately 40.5 million attempts were made to contact the IRS via its toll-free assistance lines. Assistors have answered approximately 6.3 million calls and have achieved a 72.9 percent Level of Service with a 9.6 minute Average Speed of Answer. As a result of the IRS receiving additional funding for customer service in FY 2016, the IRS is forecasting a 65 percent Level of Service for the 2016 Filing Season, which is an increase from the 38 percent originally forecasted. Overall, the IRS is forecasting a 47 percent Level of Service for the full fiscal year, which is an increase from its original forecast of 34 percent. We are currently assessing the IRS's process for allocating its Customer Service budget.

---

[8] The IRS refers to the suite of 29 telephone lines to which taxpayers can make calls as "Customer Account Services Toll-Free.
[9] The primary measure of service to taxpayers. It is the relative success rate of taxpayers who call for live assistance on the IRS's toll-free telephone lines.
[10] The average amount of time for an assistor to answer the call after the call is routed to a call center.

Second, the IRS's ability to process taxpayer correspondence in a timely manner continues to decline. The reported over-age correspondence inventory has steadily increased from 40 percent in FY 2012 to 49 percent in FY 2015. IRS management indicated that it has been necessary to focus its limited resources on maximizing taxpayer assistance on the toll-free telephone lines during the filing season while concentrating any remaining resources toward various priority programs such as identity theft and aged work.[11] In February 2016, we reported that although the IRS has taken action to improve its working of correspondence inventory, managers continue to not effectively use over-age reports to monitor and reduce inventory.[12]

Third, the IRS estimates the number of taxpayers assisted by Taxpayer Assistance Centers (TAC) will again decline this fiscal year. The IRS reported that it assisted more than 5.6 million taxpayers in FY 2015, which was a nearly 4 percent decrease from the prior year. For FY 2016, the IRS plans to assist approximately 5.2 million taxpayers, which is 7 percent fewer than in FY 2015. The IRS indicated that its strategy of not offering services at TACs that can be obtained through other service channels, such as the IRS's website, are the reasons that the IRS plans to assist fewer taxpayers at the TACs.

In July 2014, we reported that although the IRS stated that the TAC services eliminated or reduced were, in part, the result of the IRS's anticipated budget cuts, the IRS's plans did not show the extent to which the service cuts would lower the costs and the FTEs at the TACs. In fact, the FTEs allocated to TACs in FY 2014 were not substantially reduced. Furthermore, prior to making the service cuts, the IRS did not evaluate the burden each service elimination or reduction would have on taxpayers who seek assistance at the TACs.

Another challenge facing the IRS is meeting taxpayers' expectations for expanded online account access. The IRS's eventual goal is to provide taxpayers with dynamic online account access that includes viewing their recent payments, making minor changes and adjustments to their accounts, and corresponding digitally with the IRS. In a May 2015,[13] we reported that the IRS is depending even more heavily on technology-based services and external partners. The IRS continues to expand the information and tools to provide self-assistance through IRS.gov and various social media channels (*e.g.*, Twitter, Facebook, and YouTube).

---

[11] TIGTA, Ref. No. 2014-40-029, *Interim Results of the 2014 Filing Season* (Mar. 2014).
[12] TIGTA, Ref. No. 2016-40-023, *Continued Inconsistent Use of Over-age Correspondence Lists Contributes to Taxpayer Burden and Unnecessary Interest Payments* (Feb. 2016).
[13] TIGTA, Ref. No. 2015-40-053, *Taxpayer Online Account Access Is Contingent On the Completion of Key Information Technology Projects* (May 2015).

However, key information technology projects needed to provide these online options ultimately cannot be completed until the IRS allocates sufficient resources to them. The projects need to be completed to enable taxpayers to accurately authenticate their identities online, view their accounts, and communicate with the IRS using secure electronic messages. We reported that without additional funding for key information technology projects, the IRS will continue to miss opportunities to fully benefit from the cost savings and improved customer service, including reducing the reliance on traditional service channels such as telephones, paper correspondence, and face-to-face contact.

IDENTITY THEFT AND TAX REFUND FRAUD

Tax-related identify theft is a major challenge still facing the IRS. Since 2012, TIGTA has issued a series of reports assessing the IRS's efforts to detect and prevent fraudulent tax refunds resulting from identity theft. In July 2012, we reported that the impact of identity theft on tax administration is significantly greater than the amount the IRS detects and prevents. Our analysis of Tax Year (TY) 2010 tax returns identified approximately 1.5 million undetected tax returns with potentially fraudulent tax refunds totaling in excess of $5.2 billion that had the characteristics of identity theft confirmed by the IRS.[14]

We have continued to perform follow-up reviews evaluating the IRS's efforts to improve detection processes, including its implementation of TIGTA recommendations. In April 2015, we reported that the IRS continues to make improvements in its identification of identity theft tax returns before fraudulent tax refunds are released.[15] In response to our reporting that the IRS did not have a process to measure the impact of identity theft, the IRS initiated a research project in Calendar Year 2012 to develop a measurement process to assess its efforts to defend against identity theft as well as identify areas requiring additional effort. For the 2014 Filing Season, the IRS reported that identity thieves were successful in receiving approximately $3.1 billion in fraudulent tax refunds. TIGTA is evaluating the accuracy of the IRS's measurement and expects to issue its report early next fiscal year.

The IRS has implemented many of TIGTA's recommendations, and has continued in its efforts to improve its detection processes. In the 2014 Filing Season,

---

[14] TIGTA, Ref. No. 2012-42-080, *There Are Billions of Dollars in Undetected Tax Refund Fraud Resulting From Identity Theft* (July 2012).
[15] TIGTA, Ref. No. 2015-40-026, *Efforts Are Resulting in the Improved Identification of Fraudulent Tax Returns Involving Identity Theft* (Apr. 2015).

the IRS reported that it detected and prevented approximately $21.5 billion in identity theft refund fraud.

The IRS is locking the tax accounts of deceased individuals to prevent others from filing a tax return using their names and Social Security Numbers (SSN). The IRS locked approximately 30.2 million taxpayer accounts between January 2011 and December 31, 2015. For Processing Year 2015, the IRS rejected approximately 77,000 fraudulent e-filed tax returns and prevented about 16,000 paper-filed tax returns through the use of these locks as of April 30, 2015.

The IRS also continues to expand the number of filters used to detect identity theft refund fraud at the time tax returns are processed. Those filters increased from 11 filters for the 2012 Filing Season to 183 filters for the 2016 Filing Season. Tax returns identified by these filters are held during processing until the IRS can verify the taxpayer's identity. As of December 31, 2015, the IRS reported that it identified and confirmed more than one million fraudulent tax returns and prevented the issuance of nearly $6.8 billion in fraudulent tax refunds as a result of the identity theft filters.

After TIGTA continued to identify large volumes of undetected potentially fraudulent tax returns with tax refunds issued to the same address or deposited into the same bank account, the IRS developed and implemented a clustering filter tool during the 2013 Filing Season. This tool groups tax returns based on characteristics that include address and bank routing numbers. Tax returns identified are held from processing until the IRS can verify the taxpayer's identity. As of December 31, 2015, the IRS reported that, using this tool, it identified 835,183 tax returns claiming approximately $4.3 billion in potentially fraudulent tax refunds.

A new process, also implemented during the 2015 Filing Season, limits the number of direct deposit refunds that can be sent to a single bank account to three deposits. The IRS converts the fourth and subsequent direct deposit refund requests to a specific bank account to a paper refund check and mails the check to the taxpayer's address of record. In August 2015, we reported that programming errors resulted in some direct deposit refunds not converting to a paper check as required.[16]

In December 2015, Congress passed legislation that addresses TIGTA's ongoing concern about limitations in the IRS's ability to prevent the continued issuance of billions of dollars in fraudulent tax refunds. We reported that the IRS did not have timely access to third-party income and withholding information needed to make

---

[16] TIGTA, Ref. No. 2015-40-080, *Results of the 2015 Filing Season* (Aug. 2015).

substantial improvements in its fraud detection efforts. The recently enacted legislation now requires the annual filing of income and withholding information by January 31, beginning in 2017.[17] Access to this information at the beginning of the filing season is the single most important tool to detect and prevent tax fraud-related identity theft. TIGTA will be reviewing the IRS's use of the income and withholding information returns as part of its FY 2017 assessment of efforts to detect and prevent identity theft.

Identity theft also affects businesses. In September 2015, TIGTA determined that processing filters could be developed to identify business tax returns containing certain characteristics that could indicate potential identity theft cases.[18] TIGTA also reported that State information sharing agreements do not address business identity theft and that actions are needed to better promote awareness of business identity theft. The IRS agreed with our recommendations.

In order to continue to improve its detection efforts, the IRS needs expanded capabilities in its fraud detection system. The IRS's current fraud detection system does not allow the IRS to change or adjust identification filters throughout the processing year. The IRS is developing and testing a replacement fraud detection system, called the Return Review Program (RRP), which the IRS believes will provide new and improved capabilities that advance its fraud detection and prevention to a higher level.

The IRS conducted a pilot test of the RRP scoring and models during Processing Year 2014 to assess its effectiveness in identifying potential identity theft tax returns. In December 2015, TIGTA reported that although the pilot successfully identified tax returns involving identity theft that were not identified by the IRS's other fraud detection systems, it did not detect all the fraudulent tax returns identified by its existing fraud detection systems.[19]

IRS ASSISTANCE TO VICTIMS OF IDENTITY THEFT

TIGTA has identified continuing issues with victim assistance. In September 2013, TIGTA reported that, on average, it took the IRS 312 days to resolve tax

---

[17] Pub. L. No. 114-113, *Consolidated Appropriations Act, 2016.*
[18] TIGTA, Ref. No. 2015-40-082, *Processes Are Being Established to Detect Business Identity Theft; However, Additional Actions Can Help Improve Detection* (Sept. 2015).
[19] TIGTA, Ref. No. 2016-40-008, *Continued Refinement of the Return Review Program Identity Theft Detection Models Is Needed to Increase Detection* (Dec. 2015).

accounts of identity theft victims due a refund in FY 2012.[20] In March 2015, we reported that taxpayers were still experiencing long delays in resolving their tax accounts and that the IRS continues to make errors on the victims' tax accounts.[21] Our review of a statistically valid sample of 100 identity theft tax accounts resolved by the IRS during FY 2013 identified that the IRS took an average of 278 days to resolve the tax accounts and did not correctly resolve 17 of the 100 accounts (17 percent) we reviewed. We estimate that of the 267,692 taxpayer cases resolved during this period, 25,565 (10 percent) may have been resolved incorrectly resulting in delayed or incorrect refunds and requiring the IRS to reopen cases to resolve the errors.

On May 4, 2015, the IRS announced the final phase of its plan to consolidate its identity theft assistance and compliance activities into a new organization called the Identity Theft Victim Assistance Directorate. The IRS indicated that this new directorate aims to provide consistent treatment to victims of tax-related identity theft. We plan to review the IRS's implementation of this organization as part of our FY 2016 audit coverage.

Employment-Related Identity Theft

Individuals can also learn that they are victims of employment-related identity theft if they receive a notification from the IRS of an income discrepancy between the amounts reported on his or her tax return to the amount employers reported to the IRS. This can occur when an innocent taxpayer's stolen identity is used to gain employment. It can cause significant burden due to the incorrect computation of taxes and Social Security benefits based on income that does not belong to the taxpayer.

In response to a TIGTA recommendation, the IRS initiated the Employment Related Identity Theft Notification Project in 2014 to notify a test group of taxpayers that their SSNs have been used by another person for the purpose of employment. The IRS mailed approximately 25,000 letters to potential victims whose SSNs had been used on a Form W-2 accompanying a TY 2013 tax return filed by another individual with an Individual Taxpayer Identification Number (ITIN).[22] The letters also described steps the taxpayers could take to prevent further misuse of their personal information, including reviewing their earnings with the Social Security Administration

---

[20] TIGTA, Ref. No. 2013-40-129, *Case Processing Delays and Tax Account Errors Increased Hardship for Victims of Identity Theft* (Sept. 2013).
[21] TIGTA, Ref. No. 2015-40-024, *Victims of Identity Theft Continue to Experience Delays and Errors in Receiving Refunds* (Mar. 2015).
[22] The IRS created the ITIN to provide Taxpayer Identification Numbers, when needed for tax purposes, to individuals who do not have and are not eligible to obtain an SSN.

(SSA) to ensure their records are correct. However, the IRS completed the pilot in FY 2014 and did not continue issuing the notification letters to taxpayers. TIGTA is currently evaluating this pilot initiative and expects to issue its report in March 2016.[23]

IRS "GET TRANSCRIPT" DATA BREACH

On May 26, 2015, the IRS announced that unauthorized access attempts were made by individuals using taxpayer-specific data to gain access to tax information through its "Get Transcript" application. According to the IRS, one or more individuals succeeded in clearing the IRS's authentication process that required knowledge of information about the taxpayer, including Social Security information, date of birth, tax filing status, and street address.

The tax information that can be accessed on the Get Transcript application can include the current and three prior years of tax returns, nine years of tax account information, and wage and income information. The unauthorized accesses resulted in the IRS removing the application from its website. In August 2015, the IRS indicated that unauthorized users were successful[24] in obtaining access to information for over 340,000 taxpayer accounts. However, TIGTA's current review[25] of the Get Transcript breach identified additional suspicious accesses to taxpayers' accounts. Based on TIGTA's analysis of Get Transcript access logs, the IRS reported on February 26, 2016 that potentially unauthorized users were successful in obtaining access to an additional 390,000 taxpayer accounts. The IRS also reported that an additional 295,000 taxpayer transcripts were targeted but the access attempts were not successful. The IRS did not previously identify these accesses because of limitations in the scope of its analysis, including its method of identifying suspicious email accounts as well as the timeframe it analyzed.

In response to TIGTA's identification of the additional accesses, the IRS is mailing notification letters to these taxpayers and placing identity theft markers on their tax accounts, which started February 29, 2016. It should be noted that the actual number of individuals whose personal information was available to the potentially unauthorized individuals accessing these tax accounts is significantly larger in that

---

[23] TIGTA, Audit No. 201540015, *Assistance to Taxpayers Affected by Employment-Related Identity Theft*, report planned for March 2016.
[24] A successful access is one in which the unauthorized users successfully answered identity proofing and knowledge-based authentication questions required to gain access to taxpayer account information.
[25] TIGTA, Audit No. 201540027, *Evaluation of Assistance Provided to Victims of the Get Transcript Data Breach*, report planned for March 2016.

these tax accounts include certain information on other individuals listed on a tax return (*e.g.,* spouses and dependents). TIGTA plans to issue its report in March 2016.

In a report issued in November 2015, TIGTA found that when the IRS assessed the risk of the Get Transcript application, it rated the authentication risk associated with Get Transcript as low to both the IRS and taxpayers.[26] As a result, the IRS implemented single-factor authentication to access the Get Transcript application. The IRS now knows that the authentication risk was in fact high to both the IRS and taxpayers and should have required multifactor authentication. We also reported that the IRS did not complete the required authentication risk assessment of the issues Identity Protection Personal Identification Number (IP PIN)[27] application. The IRS does not anticipate having the technology in place for either the Get Transcript or IP PIN application to provide multifactor authentication capability before the summer of 2016.

TIGTA is participating in a multi-agency investigation into this matter and we have provided the IRS with some of our investigative observations to date in order to help them secure the e-authentication environment in the future.

TELEPHONE IMPERSONATION SCAM

As noted earlier in my testimony, the telephone impersonation scam has proven to be so large that it continues to be one of my agency's top priorities, and it has also landed at the top of the IRS's "Dirty Dozen" tax scams. The number of complaints we have received about this scam continue to climb, cementing its status as the largest, most pervasive impersonation scam in the history of our agency. It has claimed thousands of victims, including victims in every State represented on this committee, with reported losses totaling close to $29 million to date.

We started receiving reports of this particular phone scam in August 2013. As the reporting continued through the fall, we started to specifically track this crime in October 2013. TIGTA currently receives between 10,000 and 14,000 reports of these calls each week. To date, TIGTA has received more than one million reports of these calls. As of February 22, 2016, over 5,400 individuals have reported to TIGTA they have been victimized by this scam by paying close to $29 million, averaging over

---

[26] TIGTA, Ref. No. 2016-40-007, *Improved Tax Return Filing and Tax Account Access Authentication Processes and Procedures Are Needed* (Nov. 2015).
[27] To provide relief to tax-related identity theft victims, the IRS issues IP PINs to taxpayers who are confirmed by the IRS as victims of identity theft, taxpayers who are at a high risk of becoming a victim such as taxpayers who call reporting a lost or stolen wallet or purse, as well as taxpayers who live in three locations that the IRS has identified as having a high rate of identity theft (Florida, Georgia and the District of Columbia).

$5,300 per victim. The highest reported loss by one individual was over $500,000. In addition, over 1,275 of these victims reported that they also provided sensitive identity information to these scammers.

Here is how it works: The intended victim receives an unsolicited telephone call from a live person or from an automated call dialer. The caller, using a fake name and sometimes a fictitious employee badge number, claims to be an IRS agent. The scammers use Voice over Internet Protocol technology to hide their tracks and create false telephone numbers that show up on the victim's caller ID system. For example, the criminals may make it appear as though the calls are originating from Washington, D.C., or elsewhere in the United States.

The callers may even know the last four digits of the victim's SSN or other personal information about the victim. The caller claims that the intended victim owes the IRS taxes and that if not paid immediately, the victim will be arrested or charged in a lawsuit. Other threats for non-payment include the loss of a driver's license, deportation, or loss of a business license. They often leave "urgent" messages to return telephone calls and they often call the victim multiple times.

According to the victims we have interviewed, the scam artists made the threatening statements as described above, and then demanded that the victims immediately pay the money using prepaid debit cards, wire transfers, Western Union payments or MoneyGram payments in order to avoid being immediately arrested. The callers typically warn the victims that if they hang up, local police would come to their homes to arrest them immediately. Sometimes the scammers also sent bogus IRS e-mails to support their claim that they worked for the IRS. By the time the victims realized they had been scammed, the funds were long gone.

Over time, the scam has evolved from live callers demanding payment using prepaid debit cards to scammers using automated call dialers, or "robo-dialers," to place thousands of calls very rapidly. When the intended victim answers the phone, the automated voice states that the victim owes the IRS taxes. The victim is informed that if they do not immediately call a telephone number provided in the message, they will face arrest and possibly a lawsuit.

TIGTA has made several arrests in connection with this scam and has numerous investigations underway. While we cannot provide specific details of ongoing investigations out of concern that it will hinder our ability to prosecute those responsible, we can describe for you some of the steps TIGTA is taking to combat this scam.

To thwart scammers using robo-dialers, we have created and instituted an "Advise and Disrupt" strategy. The strategy involves cataloguing the telephone numbers that were reported by intended victims. We then use our own automated call dialers to make calls to those telephone numbers to advise the scammers that their activity is criminal and to cease and desist in their activity. As of February 24, 2016, we have placed over 48,000 automated calls back to the criminals.

Also, we are working with the telephone companies to have the scammers' telephone numbers shut down as soon as possible. Of the 541 telephone numbers that have been reported by victims, we have successfully shut down over 77 percent of them.

TIGTA is also publishing those telephone numbers determined to have been used by the scammers on the Internet. This provides intended victims an additional tool to help them determine if the call is part of a scam. All they have to do is type the telephone number in any search engine, and the response will indicate whether the telephone number has been identified as part of the impersonation scam. These efforts are producing results: our data show it now takes hundreds of calls to yield one victim, whereas in the beginning of the scam it took only double digit attempts.

In addition, TIGTA is engaged in a public outreach effort to educate taxpayers about the scam. This effort includes issuing press releases, granting interviews, issuing public service announcements, and providing testimony to the Congress. The criminals view this scam as they do many others; it is a crime of opportunity. Unfortunately, while we plan on arresting and prosecuting more individuals, the scam will not stop until people stop paying the scammers money. Our best chance at defeating this crime is to educate people so they do not become victims in the first place. Every innocent taxpayer we protect from this crime is a victory.

IMPLEMENTATION OF THE AFFORDABLE CARE ACT

The ACA provides incentives and tax breaks to individuals and small businesses to offset health care expenses, and impose penalties for individuals and businesses that do not obtain health care coverage for themselves or their employees. Implementation of these provisions will continue to present numerous challenges for the IRS in the 2016 Filing Season. For example, the IRS will continue its efforts to verify claims for the Premium Tax Credit (PTC).[28] Taxpayers who purchase insurance through an Exchange[29] are required to file a tax return and attach Form 8962, *Premium Tax Credit (PTC)*, to claim the PTC and reconcile any Advance PTC payments (APTC)[30] that were made to an insurer on their behalf. For the 2015 Filing Season, as of June 11, 2015, the IRS reported that it processed more than 2.9 million tax returns in which taxpayers received approximately $9.8 billion in PTCs that were either received in advance or claimed at the time of filing.

In a draft report issued to the IRS in February 2016,[31] TIGTA reported that its evaluation of the IRS's verification of PTC claims during the 2015 Filing Season identified that not all Exchanges provided monthly Exchange Periodic Data (EPD)[32] to the IRS prior to the start of the 2015 Filing Season as required. Without the required EPD, the IRS is unable to ensure that individuals claiming the PTC met the most important eligibility requirement—insurance was purchased through an Exchange. The IRS also cannot effectively and efficiently prevent erroneous PTC payments or ensure that the APTC paid in error is recovered.

Because it did not receive all required EPD data, the IRS developed manual processes in an effort to verify PTC claims associated with these Exchanges. However, to carry out these processes, the IRS has to suspend these tax returns during processing, which uses additional IRS resources and increases the burden on taxpayers entitled to these claims. We are evaluating the effectiveness of the IRS's verification of PTC claims during the 2016 Filing Season, including an assessment of the IRS's receipt of required EPD and Forms 1095-A, *Health Insurance Marketplace Statement*, from the Federal and State Exchanges.

In the 2016 Filing Season, the IRS must implement processes and procedures to ensure taxpayer compliance with Minimum Essential Coverage (MEC)[33] and Shared Responsibility Payment (SRP) requirements. In March 2015, we reported that the IRS

---

[28] A refundable tax credit to assist individuals and families in purchasing health insurance coverage through an Affordable Insurance Exchange.

[29] The Exchange is where taxpayers find information about health insurance options, purchase qualified health plans, and, if eligible, obtain help paying premiums and out-of-pocket costs.

[30] An APTC is paid in advance to a taxpayer's insurance company to help cover the cost of premiums.

[31] TIGTA, Audit No. 201540317, *Affordable Care Act: Internal Revenue Service Verification of Premium Tax Credit Claims During the 2015 Filing Season*, draft report issued February 2016.

[32] The ACA requires Exchanges to provide the IRS with information regarding individuals who are enrolled by the Exchange on a monthly basis. These data are referred to as Exchange Periodic Data (EPD).

[33] MEC is health insurance coverage that contains essential health benefits including emergency services, maternity and newborn care, and preventive and wellness services.

had not developed these processes and procedures during the 2015 Filing Season.[34] Taxpayers, and any individual the taxpayer could claim as a dependent for Federal income tax purposes, who did not maintain MEC must either be exempted from the requirement or pay a penalty (referred to as the SRP) for each month during which MEC was not maintained. We are currently evaluating the IRS's efforts to verify taxpayers' compliance with MEC and SRP requirements.

Finally, the IRS will also have to implement processes and procedures to ensure employer compliance with ACA provisions. For example, the Employer Shared Responsibility Provision applies to employers that had an average of 50 or more full-time employees during the prior calendar year. The ACA requires these employers to report to the IRS whether they offered full-time employees and their dependents the opportunity to enroll in coverage. This reporting requirement was delayed from Calendar Year 2015 to 2016.

Employers that do not offer health insurance coverage, or offer health insurance coverage that does not meet minimum requirements, may be subject to an Employer Shared Responsibility Provision when at least one of their full-time employees receives a PTC to purchase coverage through an Exchange. TIGTA is assessing the status of the IRS's preparations for ensuring compliance with the employer mandate and the related information reporting requirements.

IRS COMPLIANCE ACTIVITIES

A serious challenge confronting the IRS is the Tax Gap, which is defined as the difference between the estimated amount taxpayers owe and the amount they voluntarily and timely pay for a tax year. Despite an estimated voluntary compliance rate of 83 percent and IRS enforcement efforts, a significant amount of income remains unreported and unpaid. In January 2012, the IRS estimated the gross Tax Gap for TY 2006 to be $450 billion.

In FY 2015, the IRS reported that it collected more than $54.2 billion in enforcement revenue, a nine percent decrease from FY 2014. This is the sixth consecutive year that the IRS has exceeded $50 billion in enforcement revenue. While enforcement revenue has remained consistent, IRS enforcement activity has decreased due to budgetary constraints.

---

[34] TIGTA, Ref. No. 2015-43-030, *Affordable Care Act: Assessment of Internal Revenue Service Preparations to Ensure Compliance With Minimum Essential Coverage and Shared Responsibility Payment Requirements* (Mar. 2015).

For example, TIGTA reported that the IRS Collection function activities showed mixed results in FY 2014.[35] The amount collected on delinquent accounts by both the Automated Collection System and the Compliance Services Collection Operations increased, while the amount collected by Field Collection decreased. The Collection function continued to receive more delinquent accounts than it closed, although the number of delinquent accounts in the Collection queue decreased, due in part to the removal of millions of accounts that were not resolved. While the use of levies increased, fewer Notices of Federal Tax Lien were filed and fewer seizures were made. Meanwhile, taxpayers' use of the offer in compromise payment option decreased for the first time in the past five years.

The Examination function conducted 11 percent fewer examinations in FY 2014 than in FY 2013. The decline in examinations occurred across almost all tax return types, including returns for individuals, corporations, and S corporations. Seventy-one percent of return examinations were conducted via correspondence. In addition to the decline in the number of tax return examinations, productivity indicators also declined. The dollar yield per hour for most return types decreased. The no-change rates increased for most types of examinations (individuals, corporations, and partnerships). Overall, the IRS reported the audit rate was 0.8 percent in FY 2015, down from 1.1 percent in FY 2010. These compliance trends are a continued cause for concern, especially given that diminished enforcement could also affect voluntary compliance over time.

The tax compliance of business and individual taxpayers involved in international transactions also remains a significant concern for the IRS. Complex transfer pricing issues and identifying U.S. taxpayers with hidden foreign assets and accounts continue to demand additional IRS resources.

As this global economic activity increases, so do concerns regarding the International Tax Gap.[36] To address the International Tax Gap, the IRS developed an international tax strategy plan with two major goals: (1) to enforce the law to ensure that all taxpayers meet their obligations and (2) to improve service to make voluntary compliance less burdensome.

---

[35] TIGTA, Ref. No. 2016-30-004, *Trends in Compliance Activities Through Fiscal Year 2014* (Nov. 2015).
[36] The International Tax Gap is the taxes owed but not collected on time from a U.S. person or foreign person whose cross-border transactions are subject to U.S. taxation.

The IRS also currently faces the challenge of implementing the Foreign Account Tax Compliance Act (FATCA).[37] FATCA was enacted to combat tax evasion by U.S. persons holding investments in offshore accounts. Under FATCA, a United States taxpayer with financial assets outside the United States is required to report those assets to the IRS on Form 8938, *Statement of Specified Foreign Financial Assets*. In addition, foreign financial institutions are required to report to the IRS certain information about financial accounts held by U.S. taxpayers or by foreign entities in which U.S. taxpayers hold a substantial ownership interest. The IRS is developing a new international system, the Foreign Financial Institution Registration System, to support the requirements of FATCA. This system is intended to register foreign financial institutions to assist in achieving the primary objective of FATCA, which is the disclosure of U.S. taxpayer foreign accounts. TIGTA reviewed the development of this system and reported that the program management control processes did not timely identify or communicate system design changes necessary to ensure its successful deployment.[38]

TIGTA found that the IRS has taken steps to provide affected stakeholders information that explains FATCA requirements and expectations.[39] However, TIGTA identified improvements that are required to ensure compliance and to measure performance for foreign financial institutions. If plans are not properly documented, implementation and performance of compliance activities could experience unnecessary delays. TIGTA also identified some limitations with the processing of Forms 8938 which could limit management's ability to make informed decisions and achieve the IRS's compliance objectives related to FATCA. TIGTA will continue to perform audit work to assess the IRS's efforts to improve compliance in this area.

TIGTA BUDGET REQUEST FOR FY 2017

As requested by the Subcommittee, I will now provide information on TIGTA's budget request for FY 2017.

TIGTA's FY 2017 proposed budget requests appropriated resources of $169,634,000, an increase of 1.41 percent from the FY 2016 enacted budget. TIGTA will continue to focus on its mission of ensuring an effective and efficient tax administration system in this lean budget environment. The FY 2017 budget resources

---

[37] Pub. L. No. 111-147, §§ 501-541, 124 Stat 71, *96-116 (2010) (codified in scattered sections of 26 U.S.C.).
[38] TIGTA, Ref. No. 2013-20-118, *Foreign Account Tax Compliance Act: Improvements Are Needed to Strengthen Systems Development for the Foreign Financial Institution Registration System* (Sept. 2013).
[39] TIGTA, Ref. No. 2015-30-085, *The Internal Revenue Service Has Made Progress in Implementing the Foreign Account Tax Compliance Act* (Sept. 2015).

requested include funding to support TIGTA's critical audit, investigative, and inspection and evaluation priorities, while still maintaining a culture that continually seeks to identify opportunities to achieve efficiencies and cost savings.

During FY 2015, TIGTA's combined audit and investigative efforts recovered, protected, and identified monetary benefits totaling over $26.6 billion, including cost savings, increased revenue, revenue protection,[40] and court-ordered settlements in criminal investigations, and affected approximately 5.3 million taxpayer accounts. Based on TIGTA's FY 2015 budget of $158 million, this represents a Return on Investment of $168-to-$1.

TIGTA will continue to expand its oversight related to cybersecurity. The proliferation of data breaches reported in recent years and the types of information available on the Internet has compromised the effectiveness of controls used to authenticate individuals when they access their account information. Providing taxpayers with more avenues to obtain answers to their tax questions or access their own tax records online also provides more opportunities for exploitation by hackers and other fraudsters. TIGTA will evaluate the changes being considered for authenticating taxpayer access to their account information; the effectiveness of controls to mitigate external and internal threats to IRS systems; the security of data file transfers to third parties; and the effectiveness of controls to address cybersecurity incidents.

TIGTA's Audit Priorities

TIGTA's audit priorities focus on assessing key areas in which the IRS faces major risks, including ACA implementation and administration; identity theft detection and prevention; risk of unauthorized access to tax account information; international tax compliance; and oversight of the tax-exempt organizations.

Implementation of ACA provisions will continue to present many challenges for the IRS. TIGTA will continue to evaluate the effectiveness of the IRS's verification of employers' and individuals' compliance with minimum essential coverage requirements and the assessment of the shared responsibility payment as well as the IRS's continued efforts to improve the verification of Premium Tax Credit claims. In addition, the ACA also requires employers and insurers to file information returns with the IRS identifying individuals to whom employers offered health insurance and indicating whether the

---

[40] Recommendations made by TIGTA to ensure the accuracy of the total tax, penalties, and interest paid to the Federal Government.

insurance offered met minimum requirements. TIGTA will assess the IRS's efforts to identify employers that do not meet ACA requirements.

Stopping identity theft and refund fraud continues to be a top priority for the IRS and for TIGTA in our oversight role. Identity theft patterns are constantly evolving and the IRS needs to continuously adapt its detection and prevention processes. The risk for unauthorized access to tax accounts for the purpose of filing fraudulent tax returns will continue to grow as the IRS focuses its efforts on delivering taxpayers self-assisted interactive online tools. Tax account information obtained through unauthorized accesses, such as the Get Transcript data breach, can be used to file fraudulent tax returns that more closely resemble a legitimate tax return, making it more difficult for the IRS to detect. TIGTA will continue to assess the IRS's efforts to detect refund fraud committed by identity thieves and authenticate individual taxpayers' identities at the time tax returns are filed and when services are provided.

International tax compliance remains a significant area of concern. We will be continuing to assess the IRS's compliance efforts in this area, including its use of the tools that the law provides to assist in its efforts. One of the most significant tools is FATCA, which mandates reporting obligations for certain U.S. taxpayers with foreign accounts and also provides for the sharing of information between the U.S. and foreign financial institutions to ensure compliance with those obligations.

Additionally, TIGTA will be auditing the IRS's implementation of the new legislative requirement to utilize Private Debt Collectors (PDCs). On December 4, 2015, the Fixing America's Surface Transportation Act (FAST Act) was signed into law. It included provisions which amend Internal Revenue Code (IRC) Sections (§) 6306 and 6307 to mandate the use of PDCs to collect inactive tax receivables. Pursuant to IRC § 306(j), TIGTA will also biannually provide an independent review of contractor performance.

Finally, OA will be continuing to provide close oversight of the IRS's tax-exempt organization program. These entities are not subject to Federal income tax, but they represent a significant aspect of tax administration.

TIGTA's Investigative Priorities

TIGTA's investigative priorities include investigating allegations of serious misconduct and criminal activity by IRS employees; ensuring that IRS employees are safe and that IRS facilities, data and infrastructure are secure and not impeded by threats of violence; and protecting the IRS against external attempts to corrupt or otherwise interfere with tax administration.

IRS employees are entrusted with the sensitive personal and financial information of taxpayers. It is particularly troubling when IRS employees misuse their positions in furtherance of identity theft and other fraud schemes. TIGTA will continue to process and investigate the complaints from taxpayers, the Congress, IRS employees and managers, as well as continue to use sophisticated data mining tools to proactively search for internal and external criminal activity that impacts the efficient operations of the IRS. This includes proactively reviewing the activities of the 56,000 IRS employees who access taxpayer accounts for an indication of unauthorized accesses that may be part of a larger identity theft fraud scheme.

Between FYs 2011 and 2015, TIGTA processed 12,176 threat-related complaints and conducted 5,971 investigations of threats made against IRS employees. TIGTA will continue to aggressively investigate individuals who threaten the safety and security of the IRS and its employees.

The recent large-scale cybersecurity incidents in which criminals were able to obtain the information of hundreds of thousands of taxpayers from IRS systems continue to be a major investigative focus for our investigators. We are in the midst of a multi-agency investigation into these incidents and we are, as able, sharing what we are learning from these investigations with the IRS.

As mentioned earlier in my testimony, TIGTA has received more than one million reports from taxpayers claiming that they were contacted by individuals impersonating IRS employees in an effort to defraud them. To date, thousands of victims have paid close to $29 million to the scammers. TIGTA will continue to investigate these crimes against taxpayers and alert the public to this scam to ensure that taxpayers are not harmed by these criminals.

We at TIGTA take seriously our mandate to provide independent oversight of the IRS in its administration of our Nation's tax system. As such, we plan to provide continuing audit coverage of the IRS's efforts to operate efficiently and effectively and to investigate any instances of IRS employee misconduct.

Chairman Boozman, Ranking Member Coons, and Members of the Subcommittee, thank you for the opportunity to share my views.

J. Russell George
Treasury Inspector General for Tax Administration

Following his nomination by President George W. Bush, the United States Senate confirmed J. Russell George in November 2004, as the Treasury Inspector General for Tax Administration. Prior to assuming this role, Mr. George served as the Inspector General of the Corporation for National and Community Service, having been nominated to that position by President Bush and confirmed by the Senate in 2002.

A native of New York City, where he attended public schools, including Brooklyn Technical High School, Mr. George received his Bachelor of Arts degree from Howard University in Washington, DC, and his Doctorate of Jurisprudence from Harvard University's School of Law in Cambridge, MA. After receiving his law degree, he returned to New York and served as a prosecutor in the Queens County District Attorney's Office.

Following his work as a prosecutor, Mr. George joined the Counsel's Office in the White House Office of Management and Budget, where he was Assistant General Counsel. In that capacity, he provided legal guidance on issues concerning presidential and executive branch authority. He was next invited to join the White House Staff as the Associate Director for Policy in the Office of National Service. It was there that he implemented the legislation establishing the Commission for National and Community Service, the precursor to the Corporation for National and Community Service. He then returned to New York and practiced law at Kramer, Levin, Naftalis, Nessen, Kamin & Frankel.

In 1995, Mr. George returned to Washington and joined the staff of the Committee on Government Reform and Oversight and served as the Staff Director and Chief Counsel of the Government Management, Information and Technology subcommittee (later renamed the Subcommittee on Government Efficiency, Financial Management and Intergovernmental Relations), chaired by Representative Stephen Horn. There he directed a staff that conducted over 200 hearings on legislative and oversight issues pertaining to Federal Government management practices, including procurement policies, the disposition of government-controlled information, the performance of chief financial officers and inspectors general, and the Government's use of technology. He continued in that position until his appointment by President Bush in 2002.

Mr. George also serves as a member of the Integrity Committee of the Council of Inspectors General for Integrity and Efficiency (CIGIE). CIGIE is an independent entity within the executive branch, statutorily established by the Inspector General Act, as amended, to address integrity, economy, and effectiveness issues that transcend individual Government agencies and to increase the professionalism and effectiveness of personnel by developing policies, standards, and approaches to aid in the establishment of a well-trained and highly skilled workforce in the offices of the Inspectors General. The CIGIE Integrity Committee serves as an independent review and investigative mechanism for allegations of wrongdoing brought against Inspectors General.

www.ingramcontent.com/pod-product-compliance
Lightning Source LLC
Chambersburg PA
CBHW080535190526
45169CB00008B/3174